I0190036

The

Awesome Life

Series

Your Awesome Life!

90 Ways To Add MORE
Awesome Every Day

Volume 3, Edition 1

Jen Appreneur and Trish Rock

Awesome PUBLICATIONS

The "Awesome Life" Series presented by Awesome Publications.com

Copyright. All rights reserved. © AwesomePublications.com

No part of this work may be reproduced or shared in any material form (including photocopying or storing in any medium by electronic means and whether or not momentarily or incidentally to some other use of this publication) without the written permission of the copyright holder except in accordance with the provisions of the Copyright, Designs and Patents Act 1988.

Applications for the copyright holder's permission to reproduce any part of this publication should be made to the Publisher.

The purpose of this book is to entertain and educate by considering the experiences of others. You should always rely on your own independent professional advice before undertaking any new venture. No warranties or assurances, guarantees or representations about the accuracy, reliability or timelines or otherwise of the information contained in the book can be given. To the fullest extent permitted by law, Awesome Publications (including the authors and editors) shall not be liable (including liability for negligence) for any loss or damage arising out of your use of this book. You should always consider the appropriateness of the information in this book having regard to your relevant personal circumstances.

All events and scenarios in this book are based upon the author's and/or contributor's experience and are true and correct at the time of writing. Some contributions have been

sourced openly from public information sites on the internet.
No claims or warranties or ownerships or royalties are or shall
be paid.

Published and Distributed by Awesome Publications,
www.AwesomePublications.com

PO Box 544 Williamstown Victoria 3016 (Melbourne)
Australia

Phone: +61 3 9397 3975
Facsimile: +613 9397 3394
Email: info@awesomepublications.com
Website: www.AwesomePublications.com

ISBN: 978-0-9925428-2-5 (paperback)

ISBN: 978-0-9925428-3-2 (ePub)

KIVA.ORG
loans that change lives

In an effort to support self-sustainability,
innovation and entrepreneurial creativity, we
fund Kiva loans. Join our team and help change
lives, for as little as a $25 loan. More info at:
www.kiva.org/team/AwesomeEntrepreneurs.

DEDICATION

To Inspired Entrepreneurs and Authors all over the world who have awesome messages that improve peoples' lives.

May you live <u>your</u> inspired life in the most awesome way possible and remember…celebrate everything!

TABLE OF CONTENTS

Join our
"Awesome Source"

INSPIRED NEWS

Mail list

90 Days <u>FREE</u> Membership
SPECIAL OFFER for you!

Go to

www.AwesomeSourceNews.com

Right Now

FOREWORD

How Two '*Clazy-Ladies*' Made <u>AWESOME</u> The New Sexy

On a train ride to a Life and Business Seminar in Melbourne, Australia, March 2014, two business colleagues and girlfriends Trish and Jen, were discussing how their (your) perspective ON life affects your experiences IN life. And that in full awareness, even the bad things that happen, if turned in to learning, possess positivity and even blessings for better-ness rather than bitterness and therefore a more vibrant and joyful life.

The idea of living from a position of positivity, knowing there's always something good that can come out of any situation was what they were really saying. They discussed the idea of *"What if we looked at everything happening in our lives as being awesome ... eventually?"* That would mean there was always reason to celebrate and always opportunities to be grateful. It's all actually just a matter of conscious choice to create an inner energy or sense of awesomeness.

In their inspired (and excited) state, they had a joint epiphany to share with the world - that anyone can create an awesome life simply by creating awesome energy within yourself first, which in turn improves every situation and circumstance in your outer life.

They knew they had lots of friends on social media that have lots of awesome thoughts and ideas too. So, by using online crowd-sourcing facilities, they invited everyone they knew to contribute an awesome thought to a compilation book.

The book is designed for you to use on a daily basis - to easily invoke and activate the energy of awesomeness in to your life every day. This increase in your energy will in turn, bring greater happiness (and awesomeness) to other people around you too.

The true power of activating the energy in the thoughts shared in this book is alike to a 'wave of awesomeness' sweeping across the world.

The response to this idea was overwhelming and before they knew it, the book had grown twice as big as they had originally planned so once again, they got together for a 'ride', this time over Skype and brainstormed out how to make it work now that the inclusion of other people made the power bigger than first thought.

What came out of that second meeting was what you see now, a 90 day plan to integrate and activate awesomeness in to your life.

And, as both Trish and Jen are mobile app designers, they added in an app of awesomeness (why not!) so that every day you can receive awesome thoughts right there on your mobile device. The app also includes meditations and focus visuals to help embody the thoughts of awesomeness in to your being and life.

There will be 4 Volumes produced, each being 90 ways of awesome thoughts to activate awesomeness over a full year in your life. Once you're fully activated, life will never be the same.

Well, this story and the vision do not end there. The 4 book Volumes and the mobile app form part of a much bigger plan – to help people create your *"Year of Living Awesomely"*. You can find out more about that on their website www.AwesomeSourceNews.com.

You can also find out more about their public talks and workshops and "The Year of Living Awesomely, Bus of Love Tour" on the website along with links for the mobile app, merchandise and more opportunities for you to be involved in more ways too.

For now, read the Introduction and get started on Day 1 of Your MORE Awesome Life!

PS: You may wonder about "Clazy-Ladies" in the headline – it's a term they phrased during a business trip to Thailand that they took. They will tell you it's an abbreviation for "Classy, Crazy Ladies" and every time they hear it, you'll hear a little giggle from them. And if you add AWESOME to the front of it, you'll definitely get their attention.

ABOUT THE AUTHORS / CO-CREATORS

Meet Jen Appreneur

Jen is a digital age entrepreneur and businesswoman – publishing, books, audios, videos, webinars and software on today's leading digital mediums.

These include mobile apps, social media, blogging/internet & electronic magazines.

In addition, she offers online training courses and runs regular live training events in Australia, the USA and UK too occasionally.

A successful web entrepreneur since 1996, she has owned over 150 different web businesses, selling both instant download digital products and 'on-consignment' physical products - generating millions of dollars of sales for more than a decade - a formidable record by comparison to many others offering education, tools and systems for marketing success.

Current business ventures include:

- The "Queendom of Wealth™" – A High-end Mentoring Program, Mobile App, Digital Magazine, Board game, Range of Merchandise and live networking events to teach women fast and fun ways to build financial independence and to create professional fulfillment.

- "Mobile App System™" – An app design company that ensures apps for business include and are integrated in to cash-flow systems. The business is now licensed and assists service providers to expand in to the app development industry, use an easy-to-do app-building platform.

She's also a multiple-time, international best-selling Author, a sought-after public speaker around the world and media presenter.

She says, *"A little-known secret to AWESOME business success is collaboration. An idea known by many but used effectively by only a few. This book shows you how you can do it effectively too."*

You can find out more about Jen at: www.QueendomOfWealth.com

Meet Trish Rock

Trish is an entrepreneur and a modern day businesswoman who has embraced the digital age of communication and relationship building.

In retail business since 1989, and now working online, Trish believes the key to success is the experience you can give to your customers.

She has written 2 books that teach this business philosophy as well as a home study course, audio products and a webinar series. She has also contributed to 6 books on business, social media and mindset and writes a regular column on business, marketing and mobile app technology for a global magazine and a national magazine.

Trish has won awards for design excellence as well as outstanding business achievement and growth. She is a sought after app designer and developer as well as a speaker and media presenter with a following in social media and blogging.

She says *"I believe everyone can have an AWESOME business and life if they can first believe it to be true of themselves."*

You can find out more about Trish at:
www.StrategicBusinessApps.com

INTRODUCTION

"Once upon a time I tried to be Perfect, then I realized that being Awesome was so much more fun!"

It's true! We all strive towards a version of 'perfect' in our life.

Whether it's a version of perfect we've created in our own mind, or a version imposed on you by other people in your life and/or probably a combination of both, there's a vision or idea of what you are working towards.

And sometimes, the pressure we put on ourselves in striving to achieve our idea of a perfect life is unnecessary and in fact it can actually deplete our energy or life force.

When you ponder that, it's kind of ironic isn't it – that we strive towards a vision of some ideal or perfect result in our life, yet the very process to achieve that can leave us far from fulfilled and actually, even feeling exhausted and incomplete. It's a long way from feeling awesome every day that's for sure!

When asked *"What thing about humanity surprises you the most?"* the XIV Dalai Lama answered:

"Man.... Because he sacrifices his health in order to make money. Then he sacrifices money to recuperate his health. And then he is so anxious about the future that he does not enjoy the present; the result being that he does not live in the present

or the future; he lives as if he is never going to die, and then dies having never really lived."

It's a powerful statement and a truth for many in today's fast-paced life.

And we agree with The Dalai Lama – and we thought his quote was awesome enough to be in this book!

Your life, no matter how imperfect it may seem to you is already awesome, whether you fully realize it yourself yet or not. There's so much to celebrate, including even the little things that often go un-noticed in day-to-day life.

And no matter how awesome your life may feel right now, let's say it was measured on an awesomeness scale of 1-10, this quirky little book of inspired quotes is going to help you to consciously connect with more awesomeness in more ways, each day for the next 90 days.

Over the next 90 days, we will guide through a series of inspired thoughts – ideas if you like, in the form of short quotes that have been written and submitted by awesome entrepreneurs from around the world who want to help you to increase your sense of awesomeness in each aspect, every day, of your life.

To build a greater awareness and consciousness of awesomeness, the short quotes have been organized in to Chapters in this book. Each of the seven Chapters represents a different aspect of life energy and experience and you will be invited to read one quote each day (starting with the first quote in the first Chapter) and ponder its relevance in your awesome life, as your life exists right now.

By finding the connection (the awareness), you'll raise your consciousness of celebrating that awesomeness and subsequently, allow an expansion in your conscious thoughts for more awesomeness in each of the seven life aspects or realms.

It will be like a stimulating and energizing workout for your mind that will permeate and integrate in to your heart consciousness and flow through and activate in to each and every cell of your entire body.

By working through the 90 Days with us, you will become more and more of a human embodiment of awesomeness. That's pretty exciting really and that is the very experience we have had in raising our awareness and aligning our consciousness with the life force or energy and experience of awesomeness.

The more aligned we become, through recognition of where we are at presently, the more awesomeness has opened up to us. It's quite remarkable AND a lot of fun really.

As well as having more fun, integrating celebration in to our daily life, whether it's expressed inwardly, outwardly or both, makes the idea of celebrating everything feel and become so much more natural. And it may even become obvious to you just how much the idea of celebrating everything has been missing in your life until now.

Once you connect to the energy of 'Your Awesome

Life' force, you feel so much more powerful, and you will gain a greater sense of possibility of how much more powerful you become.

These short quotes are supported by meditations and inspiration instructions in our mobile app. We encourage you to download it and use the book and the app together, to get the absolute most out of it. (More info on the accompanying mobile app is on our Other Resources page at the back of this book).

We hope you love all of what we have created for you so much that you'll continue on after these first 90 days and join us on the "Year of Living Awesomely" Project too. (More info on our Facebook Group that you are now invited to join is on our Other Resources page at the back of this book).

As mentioned above, this book contains inspired and very awesome quotes from entrepreneurs all around the globe. They have contributed their best or most favorite quotes to this book to help expand your thoughts and increase your awesomeness energy and life force.

Feel free to reach out to any or all of them, either through our Facebook community or individually. We have provided their name and a link to their website below their contribution as well as in the Bibliography.

It's time now to get started with Chapter 1 and Quote 1 to energize your current awesome thought patterns, stimulate new awesome thought patterns and release old un-awesome thought patterns to raise your awareness and align your conscious thoughts with more awesomeness.

By following the instructions below, the process will help you become a greater embodiment of awesomeness –which in turn will draw more awesomeness in to your physical life and create more awesomeness in the world.

Adding more awesomeness to yourself and to all around you is a pretty cool way to live and plenty of reasons to celebrate life!

Oh one last thing, to follow us online and connect to our work at any time, these are our two most favorite social media hash-tags:
- #awesomelife
- #celebrateeverything.

How to use this book for maximum awesomeness

There are a number of ways you can use this book, not just how we suggest. Our guideline for how to use it is based on a process to a powerful outcome.

Our process is designed to help you evolve your sense of awesomeness in your life, as it is right now through this process:

THE 'YOUR AWESOME LIFE™' ACTIVATION SYSTEM

Raise Awareness --->> Align Consciousness --->> Activate Embodiment

At the start of the day:
Open the book to the page you are currently at (use a sticky note or digital bookmark so you can easily find the next one each day).

Step 1 – Raise Awareness

- Read the quote silently to yourself at normal pace.
- Pause for 5-10 seconds and take a deep breath or two at this time
- Read the quote silently to yourself again, this time at half normal pace.

As you read it at half-pace, take notice of each word by looking at it more intentionally but still read it in a manner that allows the words to flow in to each other and form a continuing sentence or paragraph.

Do not read a word, then pause, read a word, then pause too slowly otherwise you will lose the rhythm and overall meaning. Just slow it down from your normal reading pace. If you have not read at half normal pace before, you may find this a little unusual but you will soon get the hang of it.

You can practice pace by becoming conscious of your 'normal' reading pace, your 'fast' reading pace and your 'slow' reading pace.

We often read slower to children – this is the pace you want to achieve, as if you were reading it to children. Repeat this as many times as you feel you want to or need to so that it feels like it's at a pace that's comfortable for you.

Step 2 – Align Consciousness

- Take a slow, deep breath in, hold it momentarily and then exhale at the same slower pace.
- Read the quote out loud to yourself at slow pace.
- Repeat this 2-3 times, or more if you want to. Take a slow, deep breath in and before you read it out each time.

Step 3 – Activate Embodiment

- Take out your "Your Awesome Life™" journal (or a notebook or use the notepad in the app) and write out or type the quote yourself.
- Ask yourself this question "How does this quote relate or reflect in my current life?"
- Below the quote, list at least 3 ways this quote relates or reflects in your life right now. List the ways as they spring in to your mind.

You do not need to organize your thoughts, just write them down. There are no right or wrong answers, just what comes to mind. By writing or typing them out, you create a record to refer back to later and also to build on as more ideas come to you later – and they will, later on the day of the quote and maybe at a future random time as well.

It's pretty awesome how our mind and body work together to create ideas that flow. In some cases, you may, initially, struggle to make the connection of a quote to your current life, especially if it's about something that does not appear to be in your life right now.

For example, you may not be a parent but there's a quote about parenting. This is where you expand your thinking of the definition of parenting. Parenting may mean Leadership to you – so you can think about the quote in the format of guiding yourself (self governance or parenting) or guiding/leading a business or a community (group governance). It is this expansive thinking that will help you make the connections and create the embodiment of the awesome energy of each quote.

-   Now list at least 3 new ways you can introduce the idea of the quote (the awesome energy of it) in to your life.
-   Read either to yourself silently or out loud, the 3 new ways as a sentence or paragraph, starting with *"Today I introduce 3 new ways of awesomeness. They are ……………"* (Read them in the order you have written or typed them out).

You can revisit and repeat these processes for each quote as many times on the day as you want to and of course add to them at any time over the next 90 days. You can also work on more than one quote on any one day, especially if you feel inspired or are seeking new inspiration. Just make sure you complete the process for one quote through the 3 steps before starting on the second, third and beyond.

If you have any questions or comments and especially if you have some AWESOMENESS to share with us by completing the process, please visit us at our Facebook Group. Details are in the Other Resources section at the back of this book.

Finally, if there's one message we hope to impress and leave you with, it's this:

"Life gets awesome when you make up your mind to perceive it as being awesome. Celebrate everything!"

Jen and Trish

Join our
"Awesome Source"
INSPIRED NEWS
Mail list

90 Days <u>FREE</u> Membership
SPECIAL OFFER for you!

Go to

www.AwesomeSourceNews.com

Right Now

CHAPTER 1

Awesome BEING

DEFINITION:

BEING is physical presence.

Establishing security and stability while building the foundations in business and life.

These quotes will give you an awareness and consciousness about the importance of taking grounded action to manifest material abundance, in a more awesome way.

**THE
'YOUR AWESOME LIFE™'
ACTIVATION SYSTEM**

Refer to the Introduction for full details.

Step 1 – Raise Your Awareness

Step 2 – Align Your Consciousness

Step 3 – Activate Your Embodiment.

> *For each of us we only have
> one chance for a good
> End Of Life - Let's make sure
> to plan for what we want.*

-Trypheyna McShane

THIS AWESOME QUOTE FROM:

Trypheyna McShane

www.TheEndOfLifeMatters.com

> **"**
>
> *Opportunity is missed by most people because it is dressed in overalls and looks like work.*
>
> **"**
>
> -Thomas Edison

THIS AWESOME QUOTE FROM:

Thomas Edison

en.wikipedia.org/wiki/Thomas_Edison

Happiness is not in the mere possession of money; it lies in the joy of achievement, in the thrill of creative effort.

-Franklin D. Roosevelt

THIS AWESOME QUOTE FROM:

Franklin D. Roosevelt

en.wikipedia.org/wiki/Franklin_D._Roosevelt

> 66
>
> *You can only become truly accomplished at something you love. Don't make money your goal. Instead, pursue the things you love doing, and then do them so well that people can't take their eyes off you.*
>
> 99
>
> -Maya Angelou

THIS AWESOME QUOTE FROM:

Maya Angelou

www.MayaAngelou.com

> "
>
> *Formal education will make you a living; self-education will make you a fortune.*
>
> "
>
> -Jim Rohn

THIS AWESOME QUOTE FROM:

Jim Rohn

en.wikipedia.org/wiki/Jim_Rohn

> *As long as you're going to be thinking anyway, think big.*
>
> -Donald Trump

THIS AWESOME QUOTE FROM:

Donald Trump

en.wikipedia.org/wiki/Donald_Trump

I've always worked very, very hard, and the harder I worked, the luckier I got.

-Alan Bond

THIS AWESOME QUOTE FROM:

Alan Bond

en.wikipedia.org/wiki/Alan_Bond_(businessman)

Unlearn your knowledge about what WAS working to understand what is working NOW.

-Roger Hamilton

THIS AWESOME QUOTE FROM:

Roger Hamilton
Wealth Dynamics
www.RogerHamilton.com

> 66
>
> *You only live once, but if you do it right, once is enough.*
>
> 99
>
> -Mae West

THIS AWESOME QUOTE FROM:

Mae West

en.wikipedia.org/wiki/Mae_West

You jump off a cliff and you assemble an airplane on the way down.

-Reid Hoffman

THIS AWESOME QUOTE FROM:

Reid Hoffman

en.wikipedia.org/wiki/Reid_Hoffman

"

The longer you're not taking action the more money you're losing.

"

-Carrie Wilkerson

THIS AWESOME QUOTE FROM:

Carrie Wilkerson

www.CarrieWilkerson.com

66

The way to get started is to quit talking and begin doing.

99

-The Walt Disney Co.

THIS AWESOME QUOTE FROM:

The Walt Disney Company

en.wikipedia.org/wiki/The_Walt_Disney_Company

FOCUS - Follow One Course Until Successful.

-Robert Kiyosaki

THIS AWESOME QUOTE FROM:

Robert Kiyosaki

www.RichDadCoaching.com

CHAPTER 2

Awesome FEELING

DEFINITION:

FEELING is creative connection and relationships.

These quotes will give you an awareness and consciousness about the importance of self worth, inspired creativity and making decisions while taking action from an empowered emotional position, for more awesome relationships.

THE
'YOUR AWESOME LIFE™'
ACTIVATION SYSTEM

Refer to the Introduction for full details.

Step 1 – Raise Your Awareness

Step 2 – Align Your Consciousness

Step 3 – Activate Your Embodiment.

> *A warrior's daily prayer is to have the strength to love all of herself, the courage to listen to what she is guided to do and the confidence to go out, stand tall and deliver her gifts to the world.*

-Debbie Ford

THIS AWESOME QUOTE FROM:

Heather Passant
Love, Courage and Relationship Coach
www.TheCourageRevolution.com.au

> **❝**
>
> *Be Awesome.*
> *Be Brave.*
> *Be Bold…*
> *and Live outside the square.*
>
> *There's more adventure there.*
>
> **❞**
>
> -Kawena (Gwen Gordon)

THIS AWESOME QUOTE FROM:

Kawena (Gwen Gordon)
Mentor, Psychic, Author
www.MentoringKawena.com.au

> **"**
>
> *Happiness is an attitude. We either make ourselves miserable, or happy, or strong. The amount of work is the same.*
>
> **"**
>
> -Francesca Reigler

THIS AWESOME QUOTE FROM:

Francesca Reigler

en.wikipedia.org/wiki/Francesca

> 66
>
> *Sandwich every bit of criticism between two thick layers of praise.*
>
> 99
>
> -Mary Kay Ash

THIS AWESOME QUOTE FROM:

Mary Kay Ash

en.wikipedia.org/wiki/Mary_Kay_Ash

> *Mistakes are a fact of life. It is the response to error that counts.*
>
> -Nikki Giovanni

THIS AWESOME QUOTE FROM:

Nikki Giovanni

en.wikipedia.org/wiki/Nikki_Giovanni

> "
>
> *The more you praise and celebrate your life, the more there is in life to celebrate.*
>
> "
>
> -Oprah Winfrey

THIS AWESOME QUOTE FROM:

Oprah Winfrey

www.Oprah.com

66

Life is 10% what happens to me and 90% of how I react to it.

-Charles Swindoll

THIS AWESOME QUOTE FROM:

Charles Swindoll

en.wikipedia.org/wiki/Chuck_Swindoll

If the world is cold, make it your business to build fires.

-Horace Traubel

THIS AWESOME QUOTE FROM:

Horace Traubel

en.wikipedia.org/wiki/Horace_Traubel

> *Rich people act in spite of fear. Poor people let fear stop them.*
>
> -T. Harv Eker

THIS AWESOME QUOTE FROM:

T. Harv Eker

www.HarvEker.com

> **❝**
>
> *A business has to be involving, it has to be fun, and it has to exercise your creative instincts.*
>
> **❞**
>
> -Sir Richard Branson

THIS AWESOME QUOTE FROM:

Sir Richard Branson

www.en.wikipedia.org/wiki/Richard_Branson

"

I've learned that people will forget what you said, people will forget what you did, but people will never forget how you made them feel.

"

-Maya Angelou

THIS AWESOME QUOTE FROM:

Maya Angelou

www.MayaAngelou.com

> *Your fear is 100% dependent on you for its survival.*
>
> -Steve Maraboli

THIS AWESOME QUOTE FROM:

Steve Maraboli

en.wikiquote.org/wiki/Steve_Maraboli

Join our
"Awesome Source"
INSPIRED NEWS
Mail list

90 Days <u>FREE</u> Membership
SPECIAL OFFER for you!

Go to

www.AwesomeSourceNews.com

Right Now

CHAPTER 3

Awesome WILLPOWER

DEFINITION:

WILLPOWER is energy, YOUR powerful and positive energy.

These quotes will give you an awareness and consciousness about the importance of personal power and the will to keep moving forward in an empowered and effective way so as to enjoy more innate happiness in an awesome personal identity.

THE
'YOUR AWESOME LIFE™'
ACTIVATION SYSTEM

Refer to the Introduction for full details.

Step 1 – Raise Your Awareness

Step 2 – Align Your Consciousness

Step 3 – Activate Your Embodiment.

66

Make sure to dance each and every step and not get lost by always looking to the destination.

99

-Trypheyna McShane

THIS AWESOME QUOTE FROM:

Trypheyna McShane

www.TheEndOfLifeMatters.com

"

Success is found in a place of uncertainty.

"

-Emma Perrow

THIS AWESOME QUOTE FROM:

Emma Perrow
Coach Emma
www.SimpleFitness.com.au

"

I am aware that success is more than a good idea. It's timing too.

"

-Anita Roddick

THIS AWESOME QUOTE FROM:

Anita Roddick

en.wikipedia.org/wiki/Anita_Roddick

> 66
>
> *Anything is possible if you've got enough nerve.*
>
> 99
>
> -JK Rowling

THIS AWESOME QUOTE FROM:

J.K. Rowling

www.JKRowling.com

"

Great acts are made up of small deeds.

"

-Lao Tzu

THIS AWESOME QUOTE FROM:

Lao Tzu

en.wikipedia.org/wiki/Laozi

66

Consider the postage stamp: its usefulness consists in the ability to stick to one thing till it gets there.

99

-Josh Billings

THIS AWESOME QUOTE FROM:

Josh Billings

en.wikipedia.org/wiki/Josh_Billings

66

The best way to predict the future is to create it.

99

-Abraham Lincoln

THIS AWESOME QUOTE FROM:

Abraham Lincoln

en.wikipedia.org/wiki/Abraham_Lincoln

66

*If I persist long enough
I will win.*

99

-Og Mandino

THIS AWESOME QUOTE FROM:

Og Mandino

en.wikipedia.org/wiki/Og_Mandino

66

Life has no limitations, except the ones you make.

99

-Les Brown

THIS AWESOME QUOTE FROM:

Les Brown

www.LesBrown.com

> **"**
>
> *There's no shortage of remarkable ideas, what's missing is the will to execute them.*
>
> **"**
>
> -Seth Godin

THIS AWESOME QUOTE FROM:

Seth Godin

www.SethGodin.com

> ❝
>
> *If you haven't found it yet, keep looking. Don't settle. As with all matters of the heart,*
>
> *you'll know when you find it.*
>
> ❞
>
> -Steve Jobs

THIS AWESOME QUOTE FROM:

Steve Jobs

www.en.wikipedia.org/wiki/Steve_Jobs

> *Please think about your legacy, because you're writing it every day.*
>
> -Gary Vaynerchuck

THIS AWESOME QUOTE FROM:

Gary Vaynerchuck

www.GaryVaynerchuk.com

> ❝
>
> *Sustainable wealth follows a rhythm.*
>
> ❞
>
> -Roger Hamilton

THIS AWESOME QUOTE FROM:

Roger Hamilton
Wealth Dynamics
www.RogerHamilton.com

> 66
>
> *Self-control is strength. Right thought is mastery. Calmness is power.*
>
> 99
>
> -James Allen

THIS AWESOME QUOTE FROM:

James Allen

en.wikipedia.org/wiki/James_Allen_(author)

Join our

"Awesome Source"

INSPIRED NEWS

Mail list

**90 Days <u>FREE</u> Membership
SPECIAL OFFER for you!**

Go to

www.AwesomeSourceNews.com

Right Now

CHAPTER 4

Awesome LOVE

DEFINITION:

LOVE is understanding, trust and openness towards life, yourself and others.

These quotes will give you an awareness and consciousness about the importance of the power of trust in your heart as well as forgiveness and compassion in everyday living, to enjoy a more awesome loving and balanced life.

THE
'YOUR AWESOME LIFE™'
ACTIVATION SYSTEM

Refer to the Introduction for full details.

Step 1 – Raise Your Awareness

Step 2 – Align Your Consciousness

Step 3 – Activate Your Embodiment.

66

You will create peace, harmony and love in your life, work and relationships when you are at peace, harmony and in love with yourself. The inner always precedes the outer.

99

-Connie Valentine

THIS AWESOME QUOTE FROM:

Connie Valentine

www.HolisticHealingInstitute.com

> 66
>
> *YOU are the magnificence of all the beautiful colour and energy in this Universe. YOUR heart is filled with the rainbow of LOVE. Trust in this LOVE and be who YOU choose to be.*
>
> 99
>
> -Lorraine Enright

THIS AWESOME QUOTE FROM:

Lorraine Enright

www.CertitudeLifeCoaching.com.au

> **"**
>
> *The amount of Happiness we Receive…*
>
> *Depends on the amount of Love we Give.*
>
> *The answer is as simple as that.*
>
> **"**
>
> -Kawena (Gwen Gordon)

THIS AWESOME QUOTE FROM:

Kawena (Gwen Gordon)
Mentor, Psychic, Author
www.ExpandingEnergies.com.au

> *Strive to live an inspiring & joyful existence where love, servitude, gratitude & celebration are cornerstones of your legacy that will continue to have a profound effect in peoples' lives.*
>
> -Joy T. Barican

THIS AWESOME QUOTE FROM:

Joy T. Barican

www.facebook.com/JoyTBaricanEmceeServices

If you give your life as a wholehearted response to love, then love will wholeheartedly respond to you.

-Marianne Williamson

THIS AWESOME QUOTE FROM:

Marianne Williamson

www.Marianne.com

> *You know its love when all you want is that person to be happy, even if you're not part of their happiness.*
>
> -Julia Roberts

THIS AWESOME QUOTE FROM:

Julia Roberts

en.wikipedia.org/wiki/Julia_Roberts

66

Happiness is when what you think, what you say, and what you do are in harmony.

99

- Mahatma Gandhi

THIS AWESOME QUOTE FROM:

Mahatma Gandhi

en.wikipedia.org/wiki/Mahatma_Gandhi

> *If you love what you do, you'll never work a day in your life.*
>
> -Marc Anthony

THIS AWESOME QUOTE FROM:

Marc Anthony

en.wikipedia.org/wiki/Marc_Anthony

66

Learn to love something about yourself every day.

-Roula

THIS AWESOME QUOTE FROM:

Roula

www.PicsByRoula.com

To be fully seen by somebody, then, and be loved anyhow - this is a human offering that can border on miraculous.

-Elizabeth Gilbert

THIS AWESOME QUOTE FROM:

Elizabeth Gilbert

www.ElizabethGilbert.com

Your time is precious, so don't waste it living someone else's life.

-Steve Jobs

THIS AWESOME QUOTE FROM:

Steve Jobs

www.en.wikipedia.org/wiki/Steve_Jobs

> 66
>
> *A bird doesn't sing because it has an answer, it sings because it has a song.*
>
> 99
>
> -Maya Angelou

THIS AWESOME QUOTE FROM:

Maya Angelou

www.MayaAngelou.com

"

*Too many of us are not living
our dreams because we are
living our fears.*

"

-Les Brown

THIS AWESOME QUOTE FROM:

Les Brown

www.LesBrown.com

CHAPTER 5

Awesome EXPRESSION

DEFINITION:

EXPRESSION is your voice, your message, your sound and your words.

These quotes will give you an awareness and consciousness about the importance of communicating your truth and listening deeply to enjoy a more empowered, awesome way of expressing yourself.

THE
'YOUR AWESOME LIFE™'
ACTIVATION SYSTEM

Refer to the Introduction for full details.

Step 1 – Raise Your Awareness

Step 2 – Align Your Consciousness

Step 3 – Activate Your Embodiment.

Good communication is as stimulating as black coffee, and just as hard to sleep after.

-Anne Morrow Lindbergh

THIS AWESOME QUOTE FROM:

Anne Morrow Lindbergh

en.wikipedia.org/wiki/Anne_Morrow_Lindbergh

> *The first step is you have to say that you can.*
>
> -Will Smith

THIS AWESOME QUOTE FROM:

Will Smith

en.wikipedia.org/wiki/Will_Smith

> 66
>
> *The more elaborate our means of communication, the less we communicate.*
>
> 99
>
> -Joseph Priestly

THIS AWESOME QUOTE FROM:

Joseph Priestly

en.wikipedia.org/wiki/Joseph_Priestley

"

Never be bullied into silence. Never allow yourself to be made a victim. Accept no one's definition of your life, but define yourself.

"

-Harvey Fierstein

THIS AWESOME QUOTE FROM:

Harvey Fierstein

en.wikipedia.org/wiki/Harvey_Fierstein

66

When words become unclear, I shall focus with photographs. When images become inadequate, I shall be content with silence.

99

-Ansel Adams

THIS AWESOME QUOTE FROM:

Ansel Adams

www.AnselAdams.com

"

Never dull your shine for somebody else.

"

-Tyra Banks

THIS AWESOME QUOTE FROM:

Tyra Banks

www.Tyra.com

66

I want freedom for the full expression of my personality.

99

-Mahatma Gandhi

THIS AWESOME QUOTE FROM:

Mahatma Gandhi

en.wikipedia.org/wiki/Mahatma_Gandhi

> 66
>
> *Only when I'm dancing can I feel this free.*
>
> 99
>
> - Madonna

THIS AWESOME QUOTE FROM:

Madonna

www.Madonna.com

66

It is hard enough to remember my opinions, without also remembering my reasons for them!

99

-Friedrich Nietzsche

THIS AWESOME QUOTE FROM:

Friedrich Nietzsche

en.wikipedia.org/wiki/Friedrich_Nietzsche

> *Saying no to loud people gives you the resources to say yes to important opportunities.*
>
> -Seth Godin

THIS AWESOME QUOTE FROM:

Seth Godin

www.SethGodin.com

> **"**
>
> *The goal is to provide inspiring information that moves people to action.*
>
> **"**
>
> -Guy Kiyosaki

THIS AWESOME QUOTE FROM:

Guy Kiyosaki

en.wikipedia.org/wiki/Guy_Kawasaki

> **"**
>
> *The greatest comfort is in knowing we can freely express our heart conversation and message, without the constraints of human fears.*
>
> **"**
>
> -Trish Rock

THIS AWESOME QUOTE FROM:

Trish Rock

www.AwesomePublications.com

66

*Follow your inner moonlight;
don't hide the madness.*

99

-Allen Ginsberg

THIS AWESOME QUOTE FROM:

Allen Ginsberg

en.wikipedia.org/wiki/Allen_Ginsberg

CHAPTER 6

Awesome VISION

DEFINITION:

VISION is connection. A channel of thought to higher self and inner knowing that will intuitively give you direction and answers.

These quotes will give you an awareness and consciousness about the importance of tuning in to your bigger visions and creating a more awesome connection to abundance in life.

**THE
'YOUR AWESOME LIFE™'
ACTIVATION SYSTEM**

Refer to the Introduction for full details.

Step 1 – Raise Your Awareness

Step 2 – Align Your Consciousness

Step 3 – Activate Your Embodiment.

> **"**
>
> *Awaken your Inner Divine, discover your destiny and create your legacy. Seek the hidden treasures available within you, through you and your true (higher) self.*
>
> **"**
>
> -Misty Lupinacci

THIS AWESOME QUOTE FROM:

Misty Lupinacci

www.HeroHub.org

> *We humans are 99% all the same! THAT OTHER 1%...it's where we get to be AWESOME.*
>
> *GET TO WORK on your 1%. Find it & polish it lovingly until it glows.*
>
> *IT'S YOUR DIFFERENCE. The world needs that - so find a way to share it!*
>
> -Lyn Bowker

THIS AWESOME QUOTE FROM:

Lyn Bowker
The Coaching Biz Catalyst
www.22s.com/Your-Income-Wings

"

Look with the eyes and see with the heart.

"

-Petrus Bonus

THIS AWESOME QUOTE FROM:

Petrus Bonus

en.wikipedia.org/wiki/Petrus_Bonus

"

Remember, all the answers you need are inside of you; you only have to become quiet enough to hear them.

"

-Debbie Ford

THIS AWESOME QUOTE FROM:

Debbie Ford

en.wikipedia.org/wiki/Debbie_Ford

"

Hold fast to dreams, for if dreams die, life is a broken-winged bird that cannot fly.

"

-Langston Hughes

THIS AWESOME QUOTE FROM:

Langston Hughes

en.wikipedia.org/wiki/Langston_Hughes

> "
>
> *Adopt the pace of nature: her secret is patience*
>
> "
>
> - Ralph Waldo Emerson

THIS AWESOME QUOTE FROM:

Ralph Waldo Emerson

en.wikipedia.org/wiki/Ralph_Waldo_Emerson

66

The first time someone shows you who they are, believe them.

99

-Maya Angelou

THIS AWESOME QUOTE FROM:

Maya Angelou

www.MayaAngelou.com

> **"**
>
> *It is the mark of an educated mind to be able to entertain a thought without accepting it.*
>
> **"**
>
> -Aristotle

THIS AWESOME QUOTE FROM:

Aristotle

en.wikipedia.org/wiki/Aristotle

> *The more I see, the less I know for sure.*
>
> -John Lennon

THIS AWESOME QUOTE FROM:

John Lennon

en.wikipedia.org/wiki/John_Lennon

> *There are only two ways to live your life. One is as though nothing is a miracle. The other is as though everything is a miracle.*
>
> -Albert Einstein

THIS AWESOME QUOTE FROM:

Albert Einstein

en.wikipedia.org/wiki/Albert_Einstein

"

Passion is energy. Feel the power that comes from focusing on what excites you.

"

-Oprah Winfrey

THIS AWESOME QUOTE FROM:

Oprah Winfrey

www.Oprah.com

> **"**
>
> *If you're really spiritual, then you should be totally independent of the good and the bad opinions of the world...you should have faith in yourself.*
>
> **"**
>
> -Deepak Chopra

THIS AWESOME QUOTE FROM:

Deepak Chopra

www.Chopra.com

> *The simple things are also the most extraordinary things, and only the wise can see them.*
>
> -Paulo Coelho

THIS AWESOME QUOTE FROM:

Paulo Coelho

www.PauloCoelho.com

CHAPTER 7

Awesome KNOWING

DEFINITION:

KNOWING is your energy/source connection to all things. Your gateway to enlightenment and the feeling of oneness in all life comes from this flow of energy.

These quotes will give you an awareness and consciousness about the importance of this connection for a more awesome universal perception.

THE
'YOUR AWESOME LIFE™'
ACTIVATION SYSTEM

Refer to the Introduction for full details.

Step 1 – Raise Your Awareness

Step 2 – Align Your Consciousness

Step 3 – Activate Your Embodiment.

> *I am an inspiring, creative, self-expressed AWESOME soul and my wisdom helps me consciously choose the higher road of spirit rather than the familiar path of my wounded ego.*
>
> -Heather Passant

THIS AWESOME QUOTE FROM:

Heather Passant
Love, Courage and Relationship Coach
www.TheCourageRevolution.com.au

> **"** Because God created all and all is beautiful, light, darkness, sound, silence, life and death; it`s just easier to find beauty in light than in darkness, in sound than in silence, in life than in death; but it takes somebody special to appreciate it all as well. **"**
>
> -Eduardo Bibriesca

THIS AWESOME QUOTE FROM:

Eduardo Bibriesca

www.facebook.com/EddieRocker

> "
>
> *YOU are unique as is every diamond yet like the diamond YOU shine YOUR brilliance and magnificence everywhere YOU go.*
>
> ***Keep Shining***
>
> "
>
> -Lorraine Enright

THIS AWESOME QUOTE FROM:

Lorraine Enright

www.CertitudeLifeCoaching.com.au

The dreamers are the saviors of the world.

-James Allen

THIS AWESOME QUOTE FROM:

James Allen

en.wikipedia.org/wiki/James_Allen_(author)

"

If you ask the Universe to be your partner and guide you on the path to wholeness, it will oblige.

"

-Debbie Ford

THIS AWESOME QUOTE FROM:

Debbie Ford

en.wikipedia.org/wiki/Debbie_Ford

> "
>
> *You must find the place inside yourself where nothing is impossible.*
>
> "
>
> -Deepak Chopra

THIS AWESOME QUOTE FROM:

Deepak Chopra

www.Chopra.com

> "
>
> *The Holy Grail is within you –*
> *find your Inner Treasure .*
>
> "
>
> -Jay Woodman

THIS AWESOME QUOTE FROM:

Jay Woodman

www.Radiance-Solutions.co.uk

Hope is the thing with feathers that perches in the soul, and sings the tune without the words and never stops at all.

-Emily Dickinson

THIS AWESOME QUOTE FROM:

Emily Dickinson

en.wikipedia.org/wiki/Emily_Dickinson

66

*What God intended for you
goes far beyond anything you
can imagine.*

99

-Oprah Winfrey

THIS AWESOME QUOTE FROM:

Oprah Winfrey

www.Oprah.com

Coincidence is God's way of remaining anonymous.

-Albert Einstein

THIS AWESOME QUOTE FROM:

Albert Einstein

en.wikipedia.org/wiki/Albert_Einstein

66

Don't forget to feed your spirit.

99

-Roula

THIS AWESOME QUOTE FROM:

Roula

www.PicsByRoula.com

> *You may say I'm a dreamer, but I'm not the only one. I hope someday you'll join us. And the world will live as one.*
>
> -John Lennon

THIS AWESOME QUOTE FROM:

John Lennon

en.wikipedia.org/wiki/John_Lennon

Download the

"Your Awesome Life!"

Mobile App

For 'on the go'
inspiration as well as:

Meditations to
'Activate Your Awesomeness' whenever
needed.

Available now at
iTunes, Google Play and Amazon app
stores

BIBLIOGRAPHY

Name

ADAMS, Ansel
www.AnselAdams.com

ALLEN, James
www.en.wikipedia.org/wiki/James_Allen_(author)

ANGELOU, Maya
www.MayaAngelou.com

ANTONY, Marc
en.wikipedia.org/wiki/Marc_Anthony

APPRENEUR, Jen
www.AwesomePublications.com
www.QueendomofWealth.com

ASH, Mary Kay
www.en.wikipedia.org/wiki/Mary_Kay_Ash

BANKS, Tyra
www.Tyra.com

BARICAN, Joy T.
www.facebook.com/JoyTBaricanEmceeServices

BIBRIESCA, Eduardo
www.facebook.com/EddieRocker

BILLINGS, Josh
www.en.wikipedia.org/wiki/Josh_Billings

BOND, Alan
www.en.wikipedia.org/wiki/Alan_Bond_(businessman)

BONUS, Petrus
www.en.wikipedia.org/wiki/Petrus_Bonus

BOWKER, Lyn
www.22s.com/Your-Income-Wings

BRANSON, Sir Richard
www.en.wikipedia.org/wiki/Richard_Branson

BROWN, Les
www.LesBrown.com

CHOPRA, Deepak
www.Chopra.com

CHURCHILL, Winston
www.en.wikipedia.org/wiki/Winston_Churchill

COELHA, Paulo
www.PauloCoelho.com

DICKINSON, Emily
www.en.wikipedia.org/wiki/Emily_Dickinson

EDISON, Thomas
www.en.wikipedia.org/wiki/Thomas_Edison

EKER, T. Harv
www.HarvEker.com

EINSTEIN, Albert
www.en.wikipedia.org/wiki/Albert_einstein

ENRIGHT, Lorraine
www.CertitudeLifeCoaching.com.au

FIERSTEIN, Harvey
www.en.wikipedia.org/wiki/Harvey_Fierstein

FORD Debbie
www.en.wikipedia.org/wiki/Debbie_Ford

FRANKLIN, Benjamin
www.en.wikipedia.org/wiki/Benjamin_Franklin

GANDHI, Mahatma
www.en.wikipedia.org/wiki/Mahatma_Gandhi

GINSBERG, Allen
www.en.wikipedia.org/wiki/Allen_Ginsberg

GIOVANNI, Nikki
www.en.wikipedia.org/wiki/Nikki_Giovanni

GILBERT, Elizabeth
www.ElizabethGilbert.com

GODIN, Seth
www.SethGodin.com

GORDON, Gwen (Kawena)
www.ExpandingEnergies.com.au

HAMILTON, Roger
www.RogerHamilton.com

HOFFMAN, Reid
www.en.wikipedia.org/wiki/Reid_Hoffman

HUGHES, Langston
www.en.wikipedia.org/wiki/Langston_Hughes

JOBS, Steve
www.en.wikipedia.org/wiki/Steve_Jobs

KIYOSAKI, Robert
www.RichDadCoaching.com

LENNON, John
www.en.wikipedia.org/wiki/John_Lennon

LINCOLN, Abraham
www.en.wikipedia.org/wiki/Abraham_Lincoln

LINDBERGH, Anne Morrow
www.en.wikipedia.org/wiki/Anne_Morrow_Lindbergh

LUPINACCI, Misty
www.HeroHub.org

MADONNA
www.Madonna.com

MANDINO, Og
www.en.wikipedia.org/wiki/Og_Mandino

MARABOLI, Steve
www.en.wikiquote.org/wiki/Steve_Maraboli

McSHANE, Trypheyna
www.TheEndOfLifeMatters.com

NIETZSCHE, Friedrich
www.en.wikipedia.org/wiki/Friedrich_Nietzsche

PASSANT, Heather
www.LifeHarmony.com.au

PERROW, Emma
www.SimpleFitness.com.au

PRIESTLY, Joseph
www.en.wikipedia.org/wiki/Joseph_Priestley

REIGLER, Francesca
www.en.wikipedia.org/wiki/Francesca

ROBERTS, Julia
www.en.wikipedia.org/wiki/Julia_Roberts

RODDICK, Anita
www.en.wikipedia.org/wiki/Anita_Roddick

ROCK, Trish
www.AwesomePublications.com

ROHN, Jim
www.en.wikipedia.org/wiki/Jim_Rohn

ROOSEVELT, Franklin D.
www.en.wikipedia.org/wiki/Franklin_D._Roosevelt

ROULA, Roula
www.PicsByRoula.com

ROWLING, J.K
www.JKRowling.com

SMITH, Will
www.en.wikipedia.org/wiki/Will_Smith

SWINDOLL, Charles
www.en.wikipedia.org/wiki/Chuck_Swindoll

The Walt Disney Company
www.en.wikipedia.org/wiki/The_Walt_Disney_Company

TRAUBEL, Horace
www.en.wikipedia.org/wiki/Horace_Traubel

TRUMP, Donald
www.en.wikipedia.org/wiki/Donald_Trump

TZU, Lao
www.en.wikipedia.org/wiki/Laozi

WEST, Mae
www.en.wikipedia.org/wiki/Mae_West

VALENTINE, Connie
www.HolisticHealingInstitute.com

VAYNERCHUCK, Gary
www.GaryVaynerchuk.com

WALDO EMERSON, Ralph
www.en.wikipedia.org/wiki/Ralph_Waldo_Emerson

WILKERSON, Carrie
www.CarrieWilkerson.com

WILLIAMSON, Marianne
www.Marianne.com

WINFREY, Oprah
www.Oprah.com

WOODMAN, Jay
www.Radiance-Solutions.co.uk

ZIGLER, Zig
www.Ziglar.com

OTHER RESOURCES

- **Join our "Awesome Source" Mail list (90 Days <u>FREE</u> Membership)**

Go to www.AwesomeSourceNews.com to join now!

- **Download the "Awesome Life" App**

Search "Awesome Life" or "Your Awesome Life" in App Store, Google Play and Amazon App Store

- **Listen to the "Your Awesome Life Activation Meditations" Audios**

Details on how to do that are included in the app.

- **Join the "Year of Living Awesomely" Facebook Community**

Go to www.facebook.com/groups/yourawesomelife.

- **Join our Facebook Page**

Connect with us at www.facebook.com/AwesomeAuthors.

- **Become An Author/Contributor**

Visit us at www.AwesomePublications.com.

- **Advertise In the App**

Send an email via info@awesomepublications.com.

- **Media inquiries**

Send an email via info@awesomepublications.com.

www.ingramcontent.com/pod-product-compliance
Lightning Source LLC
Chambersburg PA
CBHW061739020426
42331CB00006B/1289

* 9 7 8 0 9 9 2 5 4 2 8 2 5 *